FRANKLIN WALDEN

The Greatness of GOD

AT THE INTERSECTION OF THE NATURAL AND THE DIVINE

THE GREATNESS OF GOD
Copyright © 2000

Franklin Walden Ministries
P.O. Box 50
Jennings, FL 32053

Printed in the United States

ISBN Number: 0-939241-79-X

To my Lord and Savior Jesus Christ.
Thank You for letting me live in the greatness
of Your love and entrusting me with a ministry
of sharing it with others.

CONTENTS

The heavens declare the glory of God; the skies proclaim the work of his hands. Day after day they pour forth speech; night after night they display knowledge. There is no speech or language where their voice is not heard. Their voice goes out into all the earth, their words to the ends of the world.

PSALM 19:1-4

INTRODUCTION

God can be found in all of His creation, mankind included, if we take the time to look. God is all around us, especially in nature. And all we have to do to see, hear, and feel God is to be still. Stop and listen. Nature will teach us about its Creator and His great love.

We find His greatness in the streams, lakes, rivers, trees, and flowers. We see His greatness in the animal kingdom, the birds of the air, and the fish in the sea. We can see the greatness of His design in mankind. God made man in His image. However, mankind has hidden the image of God and His love behind a curtain of sin, greed, and hypocrisy. People say 'God is dead' but they're so wrong. Feel the rejuvenating power of a gentle rain. Stand in awe at the glory of a sunset or the majesty of the moon and stars. God can be identified through all the works of His hands!

When I walk in the woods, I feel so close to God that it's as if I am enveloped by His presence. When I smell the sweet fragrance of the flowers, it makes me mindful of His closeness. As I hear the wind blow, I remember the Holy Spirit fell upon those tarrying in the upper room as a mighty, rushing wind. The rainbow after a cooling rain reminds me of the covenant of life God gave Noah after destroying the earth by water. Standing on the banks of a river and watching it's gentle flow causes a yearning in my heart to drink from the wonderful River of Life.

I can pass through an orchard and admire the beautiful, luscious fruit growing on the trees and be reminded of the Tree of Life and the provision God made for our eternal home. The soothing murmur of a dove's coo brings me to the realization that God's peace surpasses all understanding. And the jubilant song the nightingale sings shows how the Great Master of Music brings joy to the heart of every child of God!

This is how I see God in His created nature. You can too! Bring the hectic pace of your day under control. Take a moment to see and feel His greatness all around! Be still and listen to that sweet, soft voice in your inner being. Can you hear it?

One

LESSONS OF FAITH FROM A MOCKINGBIRD

Day 1

I'm out walking in my backyard. Most of the time my backyard is just a quiet haven where I can relax or get some exercise but today I notice something unusual. A lone mockingbird is relentlessly flying back and forth from various places in the yard to my old Long Model 560 farm tractor. So I stop to watch. It doesn't take me long to realize she is building a nest under the faded plastic seat of this iron mule. The tractor hasn't seen any duty in some time so I'm not concerned about the bird's choice for her nursery. It's as good a place for the nest as any other, I think. The mockingbird is oblivious to me being in the vicinity. She works tirelessly to finish her task. And I make a mental note to revisit her new home as soon as she completes the methodical labor.

Day 3

A few days have gone by now and I remember the promise I made to check back with Mrs. Mockingbird. Without disturbing a thing, I cautiously peer into the nest and there, to my delight, are four little eggs. I can feel my anticipation rising as I purpose to keep a vigilant watch to see nature's miracle of birth. Suddenly, the mockingbird appears. She flies to the top of the smokestack of my tractor and sings her heart out. I pause a final moment before leaving. I love to hear a mockingbird sing. And in this moment I hear the Lord speaking to my inner man that she is singing to Him of her happiness at becoming a mother.

Day 6

It's a new morning, but I'm not feeling well. And to top it off, someone is coming to borrow my tractor today. My concern for the mockingbird and the care of her nest grows with each passing moment. So when the man arrives, I tell him about the nest and those four eggs. I tell him about how this feathered mother watches over her tiny treasure and sings her joy for anyone who will listen. Even though the man doesn't share my emotional attachment, he carefully moves the nest from under the seat and places it close to the nearby fence. He's sure the fence and the wisps of tall grass will provide the nest some protection but as the outdated tractor springs to life and he drives away, I sit there with an empty feeling in my stomach. My thoughts are interrupted as I look up and see that mother bird observing the whole scene from a lanky, pine tree. Can a bird look sad? For just an instant I thought I could see it in her eyes. What if I had that kind of loss in my life, I ask myself. How would I cope? But then His still, small voice resonates in my spirit; *"Watch, and you can learn from the mockingbird."*

As I'm struggling with my emotions, the mother bird breaks out in song, as if everything in her world is okay. Meditating on this chain of events, I realize the loss of her home and family has not changed her attitude toward

God or life. I decide to join the mockingbird in praising God. And then I notice something else. My day has brightened. A smile appears on my face. I'm feeling better now.

Day 7

There's renewed activity in my backyard today. The mockingbird is on the move again. She's depositing bits of straw to the grapevine. Is the preacher in me becoming a bird-watcher? I'm going to slip out later and take a peek at the new nest.

It too, has four eggs in it! And over the course of the following weeks, she sits on those eggs in all kinds of weather. Day after day, hot or cold, rainy or dry, nothing seems to bother her. The only time I catch her leaving her sanctuary in the grapevine is when she flies to the top of the fencepost and shares a song with the rest of the world.

Day ? *(I know; I should be keeping track!)*

I've lost count of how many days it's been now. But I decide it's time for another peek. My curiosity is rewarded. Two of the eggs have hatched. I'm so proud of that mother bird. Even when she had lost (what I considered) her all, she never gave up or quit singing. She patiently started over again and continued to praise God the whole time. The still, small voice I heard was right. I had learned a valuable lesson. The mockingbird had taught me to keep on singing. No matter what my losses or even if I hit rock bottom; if I keep singing, I'll have the strength to start over again.

A Week Later

A bad storm has come up today. The wind is howling, the tops of the trees are dancing uncontrollably, wave after wave of thunder rolls toward the house, and lightning cracks across the windowpanes. But my thoughts and concerns are not for my safety or the threat of possible damage to my home. I'm thinking about Mother mockingbird and her helpless babies in the nest clinging to the grapevine. I rush over to the back window to see if I can catch a glimpse of their fate through the storm.

Much to my surprise, there's hardly a leaf moving anywhere on that vine! In the middle of the storm, the grapevine is providing a safe refuge for this little family. I'm struck with the awesome assurance that God is our peace through every tempest of life. Watching all that this mockingbird has gone through and the hardship she's endured gives me courage and renewed strength. God has reinforced a powerful truth in my heart:

> *This is the day the Lord has made; let us rejoice and be glad in it.*
> PSALM 118:24

I will always praise God for His greatness. I will praise Him for the way He loves and watches over His children every day. We can know this side of God if we just accept the evidence our five senses relate to us about His creation. Discovering God in His creation causes life to become more beautiful each day. God wants us to enjoy all His creation. Be thankful for His blessings. Let your soul sing out in praise to the Lord and give Him glory!

Two

"CAN THIS LITTLE BIRD FLY?"

I've learned quite a bit about God's greatness in my lifetime. And through His love, I've learned to be kind to all people as well as animals and birds. I never intentionally hurt any creature and if I find them hurt, I try to help them.

Some time ago I was in Toronto, Canada conducting a revival. I was staying in a motel near Lake Ontario. One afternoon I decided to take my Bible and sit at a picnic table down by the lake, to read and study for the evening service. Walking down to the shore, I noticed a little sparrow fluttering on the ground. It was hurt and couldn't fly. Out of the corner of my eye I spotted a large, yellow cat slinking toward its fallen prey. I knew if I didn't do something quick, the cat would kill this helpless bird.

In an instant I held the quivering creature in my hand. But what should I do now? The immediate danger had passed but the lingering question remained. I walked down to the edge of the water and stood there for a moment contemplating my dilemma. And then I heard Him. My inner man echoed back His words... *"Can this little bird fly again?"* I answered, "Lord, You know."

And so, I extended my hand to the heavens, to the God whose eyes are upon the sparrow and I prayed a simple prayer. I uncurled my fingers and the sparrow took flight over the banks of Lake Ontario. The bird made a staccato path out over the lake and back again; twice and then a third time. Finally, it flew directly over my head and chirped. If I understand bird language, I interpreted it to be a grateful "thank you!"

Our God is truly a God of greatness!

Three

GOD MAKES A WAY FOR A WILLING HEART

God's qualities are higher than all creation and yet, He makes Himself known to mere mortals. Through the Bible, we know Him as the great I AM, the All-Supreme, and the Father who knows the desires of our heart. He is identified as the All-Sufficient One who provides for our needs as long as we remain in His righteousness.

Our annual camp meetings in Moultrie, Georgia have attracted ministers throughout North America. This particular camp meeting was no different. We were all enjoying each other's fellowship and every night, one or two would take a few minutes to share with those in attendance. One night, a minister from Mexico stood to speak. He told of the great need in his native country. Transportation was required to go deep into the mountain regions to share the gospel. Money was needed for Bibles and to build churches so the new converts could be taught to grow in the faith.

I listened closely. I had a desire to help, but my desire was a lot bigger than my wallet. I needed a financial miracle, too. But the desire to help wouldn't leave me. For several days it lingered on my heart. So I prayed and told the Lord if I had a hundred dollars, I would give it to this minister from Mexico to help in his outreach. At that time, a hundred dollars was a lot of money. It might as well have been a thousand. The chances of getting it were very slim.

Then one day my car needed a front-end alignment. I happened to have a friend who had a tire and alignment shop in Moultrie and I knew he would do the necessary adjustments to my car and let me pay him for his services later. My friend was not "born-again" but he did have a great respect for Christians. I took my car into his shop and he said he would be happy to take care of the problem. He instructed the mechanics to place my automobile on the rack right away. Then he turned and walked across the road to where his tire re-capping center was located, leaving me standing in front of his shop. I saw him looking at some old tires and it occurred to me to say a quick prayer for the Lord to save him. Almost at the same time, my mind drifted back to the minister from Mexico. I wound up my prayer by saying, "And Lord, I sure wish I had that hundred dollars to give him before he leaves to go back to Mexico."

I looked up. My friend had started back across the road to where I was standing. He walked up to me and said, "Preacher, here's a hundred dollars. It's not for you. I want you to give it to a minister in Mexico." Without another word, he turned and crossed the road again to resume what he was doing!

In God's greatness, He always makes a way for those who have a willing heart. This man, although a sinner, was in touch with God. God was able to use him. If we were all as "tuned in" as this man was, we would know Him in the quality of His greatness. The Lord reads our hearts. He doesn't regard the stature or appearance or social position of the outer man (1 SAMUEL 16:7b).

Later on, I had the privilege of praying for this individual and saw him surrender his life to Christ and be saved. It brought to mind the scripture which says,

> *What, after all, is Apollos? And what is Paul? Only servants, through whom you came to believe - as the Lord has assigned to each his task. I planted the seed, Apollos watered it, but God made it grow. So neither he who plants nor he who waters is anything, but only God, who makes things grow. The man who plants and the man who waters have one purpose, and each will be rewarded according to his own labor.*
> I CORINTHIANS 3:5-8

Four

HIS GRACE
IS SUFFICIENT

In 2 CORINTHIANS 12:7-10 we read of Paul's struggle and prayer to be delivered from what he called "a thorn in my flesh." The Lord responded to this apostle with the words,

> *My grace is sufficient for you, for my power is made perfect in weakness.*
> 2 CORINTHIANS 12:9A

In the greatness of God we will always find God's grace is sufficient for every one of our needs. And when God speaks, He has a reason for saying it. He doesn't waste words. He comes straight to the point. If we are obedient to His command and obey Him without question, He will manifest His greatness.

One fall, I was seeking the Lord to determine where to set up my big, gospel tent for revival meetings. While in prayer, I felt impressed by the Spirit to go to Lakeland, Florida. The necessary arrangements were made and the tent was erected the latter part of November. Almost as soon as the last anchor was in place, the weather turned bitter cold. It even snowed! The surrounding orange groves were devastated as the freeze hit. We had space heaters under the tent but only fifteen people braved the unusual weather to attend the first service. And most of them were my friends.

We had spent virtually all the money we had in setting up this meeting and the tent so we were stuck. But we had to do something. I have never doubted God's leading so I knew He had sent me there for a reason, even if I didn't know what it was. I began to talk with my heavenly Father just as a child would talk to their earthly father when they need an answer to a problem. After praying, I felt we should take the tent down the next day and leave Lakeland.

The shadows had lengthened and evening stretched into night. My friends and I were huddled around one of the heaters for a Bible study. The tent flap rustled and a disheveled man peered inside. It was obvious he had come just hoping to get out of the cold. And in the next few moments it was also obvious he was a wino and hurting. Evidently, he had slipped and fallen and broken his arm.

My faith was strong. I began to witness to him about Jesus and God's abounding love. I took the opportunity to lead him to the Lord and after he prayed the sinner's prayer, I asked him if he believed the Lord could heal his broken arm. You could see and feel where the bone was sticking up under the skin. His response was "yes" and my friends and I prayed the prayer of faith. The bone went back into place! God had instantly healed the converted wino! He left rejoicing and praising God.

The next day we took the tent down, loaded it on the truck, and transported it to my friend, Brother Dennis Holt in Clearwater, Florida. By now it was getting close to Christmas and we didn't have money to get back to Georgia. All we had was a Gulf credit card to buy gas. My daughter Newana was only a three-month-old infant. It was a worrisome situation but I've always trusted God. So my wife, my daughter, and I headed out in faith. We didn't have a home to return to in Georgia but we did have family and friends we could stay with there. After we got back to Georgia, some of our friends began to question whether or not I had really heard the Lord in going to Lakeland with the tent. I could only reply, "I know the voice of God and I know I was in His will."

A friend gave us ten dollars for Christmas. Then God moved on the heart of a nurse to let us move in with her for the winter months. She provided us with free room and board. We went on with our lives and our ministry but every once in a while I would wonder what happened to that old wino who had come to the tent in Lakeland.

The Lord knew my heart's desire. A year later in Atlanta, I ran across a man who had been saved and delivered from a wasted life as an alcoholic hobo. I introduced myself to this man and he asked, "Are you the same Preacher Walden who set his tent up last November in Lakeland?" I said, "Yes!" He continued by telling me a thrilling story. The old wino I had led to Christ and seen healed of a broken arm twelve months earlier had made his way to the infamous Hobo Jungle in Tampa, Florida. It's a place where homeless winos and vagrants hang out. The converted wino began to witness to these displaced individuals about all that had happened to him under the tent. He told them of the power of Jesus. This man concluded by telling me, "I was one of the winos who got saved that night. That guy is going all over the country preaching and teaching about Jesus and the greatness of God. God is blessing his ministry and he's reaching many homeless for the Lord!"

Now, if I had not obeyed God and gone to Lakeland, Florida for that one night, many people might have missed God. We never know what God has in store when He tells us to do something. But we can be sure He knows what He is doing. God's grace is sufficient and we should never question His motives or reasons. We may not understand or comprehend His doing, but if we obey in faith, we will see the greatness of a mighty God. He is the God of all creation and we can have a relationship with the All-Sufficient One!

Five

CLOSE EN'COW'NTERS (OF THE FOUR-LEGGED KIND)

God not only provided healing for man and woman but when Jesus took those stripes on His back before going to Calvary it was to destroy all sickness and disease and to deliver us from the curse of the Law. I learned this as a young boy growing up with my mother and father. They were people of great faith. I can remember my dad praying for the sick. I never got tired of watching the miracles take place when dad prayed for his family, friends, neighbors, even his livestock!

We had set the tent up in Adel, Georgia. Souls were being saved and people with all kinds of sickness and diseases were being miraculously healed by the power of God. The tent was filled to capacity every night. One night a farmer stopped me as I was leaving the tent. "I need to talk to you," he implored. I don't usually tell people where I am staying when I am in revival because I feel most of my time should be taken up in praying and studying God's Word. But there was something about this man that made me want to hear what he had to say. I told him to come to my motel the next day.

When he arrived that morning, he seemed hesitant and uncertain of how to tell me what was on his heart. So I encouraged him, "Brother, just tell me whatever it is you need to talk to me about and maybe God and I can help you." Reluctantly Brother Crosby explained he was unmarried and lived with his mother about five miles outside Adel. He shared how he had taken care of his mother since his father had passed away and how they made a living from their little farm. And then he began telling me about their old milk cow. She had borne them many calves for beef and milk. Now, over twenty years old, the veterinarian had given them the sad news that she had cancer on one of her teats and suggested she be put to sleep.

The farmer was really upset about her condition. "I just can't stand the thought of her dying," he said. "Preacher, I've watched you pray for people under the tent and seen God heal them. I know she's just an old milk cow but do you suppose maybe God would heal her? He made her and I just wondered if it would be asking too much for you to come out to the farm, meet my mother, and pray for her and our cow."

How could I say "no?" I agreed to come out to the farm the next day. That night and into the following morning it rained. The skies were an ominous gray and everything was drenched from the soaking. But as we arrived at the farm, the sun began piercing through the clouds. I met briefly with this man's mother and had prayer with her. Then we proceeded out to the barn to see the cow.

There were other animals in the barn lot and he pointed out the animal he was so concerned about. He reminded me the vet was coming in a few days to put her to sleep. I dutifully rolled up my pants legs and trudged through the mire and standing water. My mind drifted back to when I had seen my dad take his little oil bottle that he used to anoint people and his livestock, so I did what he had done many times. I took my little bottle of anointing oil out of my coat pocket and anointed that bovine between the horns and prayed the prayer of faith. Brother Crosby thanked me and I headed back to the motel. Inside, I felt I had done the right thing by praying for the cow regardless of how the situation turned out.

The revival was scheduled to close in just a few days and I knew the vet was supposed to come to check on the animal. Even though I was curious about the outcome, I was more caught up with the miracles happening under the tent. I was hoping Brother Crosby would come back and tell me what had transpired. Friday night came and still there was no sign of the farmer.

Saturday morning, a smiling and happy man met me at my motel room. The veterinarian had come to put the diseased cow to sleep, but upon examining her milk sack, the cancer had vanished. The teat looked as normal as the others. She had been healed! And once again, she was providing milk for a grateful farmer and his mother.

God is a good God and all the works of His hands are good.

Six

WRONG NUMBER, RIGHT CALL

Nowhere do we welcome God's greatness more than in the middle of life's toughest challenges. When faith is being tested and the future looks dim, the greatness of God brings us hope.

And we know that in all things God works for the good of those who love him, who have been called according to his purpose.

ROMANS 8:28

In his heart a man plans his course, but the Lord determines his steps.

PROVERBS 16:9

I'm on the phone trying to call a fellow minister about some church business. The number is long distance so I'm double-checking the digits as I dial. The connection is made and I hear the obligatory rings. The voice on the other end offers an inquisitive "hello" but I don't recognize it. It doesn't sound anything like the party I'm trying to reach. So I offer, "Is this Brother Williams?"

"No," is the voice's only reply.

"Well," I stutter, "I'm a minister and..."

I hear crying on the other end. The voice beseeches, "Can I talk to you?"

"Sure," I respond.

I discover through his tears, he too is a minister. But his life had taken some tragic turns and it caused him to backslide. Now he was trying to come back to the Lord but it seemed God didn't hear his prayers. He feels forgotten and forsaken, even by God.

"I've just made up my mind that if something doesn't happen quick, I'm going to take my life and end it all. I can't live like this. I need help. I've asked God to forgive me, but I'm not sure He has. I don't want to go to hell. Can you help me?"

I'm ready. "Do you believe God re-directed this call to you although I was trying to reach someone else?"

"Yes, I do!" I hear him say. And I hear new hope in the voice. "Then believe God has heard your prayer!" I declare emphatically as I pray for him. And God, through His mercy and grace, touches this wayward preacher and destroys the yoke of bondage that had been strangling his life. The great God who cares has set another one free!

I hang up, still rejoicing, and immediately dial the same number. I get Brother Williams on the first ring. I've just learned God has power even over the phone lines.

Seven

THE RABBIT
IN ATTENDANCE

It happened during camp meeting in Canada one year. Every evening I would go down in the field near Catfish Creek and pray. Brother Charlie always went with me. And every day for a week, I noticed an additional visitor. Just about the time we would start our prayer meeting, an inquisitive rabbit would hop out of the bushes and sit, nose twitching and ears perked and attentive. He would take an occasional nibble of grass and listen until we finished praying. Then he would disappear into the underbrush.

The camp meeting was coming to an end and this was our last day to go to our makeshift retreat and talk to the Lord. Walking to the spot, the Holy Spirit directed my attention to a lone hawk, perched silently on the limb of a dead tree. I mentioned it to Brother Charlie. He informed me the hawk had been keeping a vigil there every day, watching the little rabbit. This predator had been cautiously biding time, waiting for the precise opportunity to swoop down and capture it's next meal. Evidently, the rabbit knew his enemy wouldn't chance an attempt as long as we were nearby.

Like all the other times in the week, out popped our furry friend as we knelt down to pray. The rabbit listened. The wily hawk stood poised and waiting. When we finished, the rabbit seemed to sense this would be our last meeting together. With a final glance, he turned his little head aside as if to say, "I've enjoyed every one!"

As Brother Charlie and I walked from our precious meeting site, the hawk decided now was the time to strike. On an invisible line, it made one swift dive. Even with a week's worth of calculated intent, the hawk missed its targeted feast. Our nosey guest had escaped!

God's grace is sufficient! He kept the little rabbit in a place of safety during those prayer meetings. Now, if people could just remember that there is safety from the enemy when they pray. We would, no doubt, have more in attendance.

Eight

HIS EYE IS ON THE SPARROW

Back in 1968, I went to Brazil on a missionary trip. While there, I contracted a virus and almost died. My weight plummeted from 212 to 127 pounds. Over the next nine months I passed over one thousand gallstones. It took me over three years to be completely restored in my health. During this period of time, I stayed home and founded a church in Conyers, Georgia. Pastoring proved to be a wonderful experience but my heart was on the road in evangelism. One day, my soul was crying out to God to get well and go back on the evangelistic field. Sitting at my kitchen table looking out the screen door, I could see my dad under the shade tree next door. I thought to myself, "I'll walk over and talk to dad for awhile."

I had to sit there a few more minutes gathering my strength before I could even make it to the door. Then, something strange happened. A tiny sparrow flew by and landed on the screen door, chirping incessantly. The Spirit whispered deep into my soul, *"the eyes of the Lord are upon the sparrow."* From that moment on I knew His eyes were upon me, too.

Shortly, the sparrow whisked off and I went up to talk to dad. We began sharing about the goodness of God. I will always remember what dad said next. "Son, the Lord is going to bring you through," he intoned and looking back now it was a word of prophecy. Those words brought renewed strength to my spirit. About that time, I looked back toward my house to the bedroom where I had spent so many painful and restless nights. There on the window screen sat the sparrow, chirping and fluttering its wings as if it didn't have a care in the world. I took it as a sign that God had everything in His control and I didn't have to worry. Dad prayed the prayer of faith for me and I was so confident I was healed that I went home and told my wife to start packing; we were going to Canada to preach. We left the following day for Aylmer, Ontario.

We had started a church in Aylmer but construction was moving slowly. Only the basement had been completed but we were having services there. Just three days after we arrived, I took a serious turn for the worse. I thought I would die as I passed twelve more gallstones. I couldn't understand what had happened. I knew when dad prayed God had touched me but here I was sick again. I needed to talk with my heavenly Father.

There was only one door into the basement of the unfinished church. I shut myself inside and began pacing the length of the floor, back and forth, crying out to the Lord. An hour passed and still I was trying to gain an audience with God. "Please Lord," I begged, "I need You to speak to me." I stopped my pacing. I stood still with my eyes closed and waited.

"Open your eyes." I acknowledged His voice speaking to my inner man. When I did, there was a sparrow directly in front of me, fluttering and chirping. The Holy Spirit engulfed me and I began praising the Lord. I was so happy! All my pain left! God had touched me and I was healed again. If we learn to listen, there are many ways God can speak to us. His greatness is everywhere if we will just recognize it.

> *Are not two sparrows sold for a penny? Yet not one of them will fall to the ground apart from the will of your Father. And even the very hairs of your head are all numbered. So don't be afraid; you are worth more than many sparrows.*
> MATTHEW 10:29-31

Not only is He mindful of the sparrow, the Bible tells us He is touched by the feeling of our inadequacies and weaknesses.

> *For we do not have a high priest who is unable to sympathize with our weakness...Let us then approach the throne of grace with confidence, so that we may receive mercy and find grace to help us in our time of need.*
> HEBREWS 4:15A,16

God is so great; He doesn't change over the years. His Word pronounces,

> *Jesus Christ is the same yesterday and today and forever.*
> HEBREWS 13:8

Nine

HEALER

I had been away from home for some time in revivals. I hadn't seen or talked to my mother in this duration so I came home for a visit and to have services in the local church. Souls were being saved and miracles were taking place in the meetings each night. It was the last night and the power of the Holy Spirit filled the sanctuary.

I had already prayed for many people and was about to leave the platform when the Holy Spirit turned me around. I called my mother to the front. I said, "Mom, the Lord just spoke to me that He is going to heal you tonight!" At the time, mom had not told me what was wrong or if anything was wrong with her. I prayed the prayer of faith for my mother.

After the service, I asked her to ride home with me. She feared she had breast cancer. Since I was a breast-fed baby I asked if I could see the cancer. The mammary gland had a hole in it about the size of a grape. It was swollen, with red streaks coursing through the breast. It was an awful sight. Mom hadn't told anyone but my sister about her condition. And she had told her only that very evening before the service. Mom had prayed that if God was going to heal her, to let her son call her out of the audience by the revelation of the Spirit. It was a confirmation of what the Lord was about to do for my mother.

As I looked at the breast I had nursed as a child, the Spirit came over me again and I proclaimed, "Mom, you are healed!" She left to go home and the next morning there was just a speck about the size of a match head on her breast. Soon, even that was gone!

> *He himself bore our sins in his body on the tree, so that we might die to sins and live for righteousness; by his wounds you have been healed.*
> 1 PETER 2:24

God keeps His promises. I saw the manifestation of this scripture in my own mother. Praise God!

Ten

GOD
ISN'T FORGETFUL

When I think of God's greatness, I can't help but
ponder where He brought me from and where I am today.
I can't forget how God has walked with me. At times He's
been right by my side and many times He's carried me but
never has He forgotten or forsaken me in my time of need.
God has sealed His faithfulness to us with this promise.

*God is not unjust; he will not forget your work and the
love you have shown him as you have helped his people
and continue to help them.*
HEBREWS 6:10

We had been in Cambridge, Ontario Canada for
eighteen days. The tent was filled almost every night. I was
preaching and praying for the sick. People were being
healed. I remember a nurse from London came up for
prayer. She had been forced to quit her career because she
had a hole in her heart. Her appeal was, "If God would heal
me I would be so grateful. The doctors have said I'll never
live a normal life. They don't know how long I can live in
this condition. But I want to live for God. I want to get

married and have children." I laid hands on this nurse and asked the Lord to grant her petition. In that instance, she was healed. Today she is married and has grown children of her own.

But in spite of all that was happening in this meeting, I did not feel the anointing of the Lord...not even for one night. All I could do was obey the Word and fight the enemy day and night. I called upon the Lord but I could not feel His presence. It was an intense trial of my faith.

On the last day of this tent revival, Brother Jack Thomas and his family came down from Toronto. This precious man is the secretary of the Franklin Walden Evangelistic Association and has served in this ministry with me for over thirty years. Before the evening service began, I got in the car with this man and asked him to drive away from the tent because I needed to talk. We drove a few hundred yards and stopped. And I began to pour out my heart. I shared how I had not been able to feel God's anointing during this entire ordeal. I couldn't contain the tears and began to weep on his shoulder. Regaining my composure, I started to apologize. He took me by the hand.

"Brother Walden, everybody needs a shoulder to cry on sometimes," he said.

His words struck a powerful chord in my spirit. From that moment on I committed to make my shoulder available to anyone who needed some strength.

We drove back to the tent and I really thought I would feel God's Spirit that night. It was not to be. After

I preached and prayed for the sick, I was about to dismiss the service when suddenly I began to prophesy. The prophecy said there would be a flood in the city. I foresaw cars floating down the street and extensive damage to the city's homes and businesses. The editor of the local newspaper was present and wrote down the prophecy as it came forth. Three weeks later, the fateful event took place just the way the Lord said it would. The newsman wrote in his editorial, 'God sent His servant to our city and we did not receive him.'

Over the course of those eighteen days, I learned there are times when we have to live and walk solely on the basis of faith. It taught me God is always there, whether I feel the Spirit or not. All I have to do is act on His Word in faith because God is faithful to remember us.

Eleven

ANGELS

We left Cambridge and began a revival with Dr. Alex Ness at the Christian Center in Toronto, Ontario. The meeting commenced with several souls saved and the sick being healed. I experienced the greatest anointing of the Spirit I have ever had.

In this beautiful edifice, they had hung 20-foot multi-color drapes as a backdrop to the platform area. The sanctuary contains no windows. One night the church was filled to capacity. After my message, I began praying for the sick. One hundred fifty people crowded into the prayer line. Exactly one hundred fifty people were touched and healed by the power of Almighty God! During this Spirit's demonstration of healing and miracles, those large, stationary drapes began rippling. People saw the angels of the Lord appear on the platform with me!

One young lady had come up for prayer for her shoulder. The shoulder would continually pop out of joint. Doctors would reset it but it wouldn't remain in place. As I prayed, the shoulder went back into its proper position! As this happened, a scream erupted from someone sitting in the middle of the congregation. Church ushers rushed to see what was wrong. A phenomenal story began unfolding. The young lady who had just been healed of the displaced shoulder had brought a friend to the service. This friend was fearful because she had never before been in and experienced a healing service. This woman was in need of a miracle herself. Her pregnancy had brought on unexpected complications and her doctor had informed her the baby she was carrying was dead. Surgery was scheduled to remove the still fetus.

The lady whose shoulder was healed had been praying, "Lord, when you heal my shoulder, resurrect the baby in my friend's womb." At the exact moment God performed the miracle in the shoulder, the baby leaped to life inside the womb of her friend! This was the first movement in five months according to this expectant mother!

Yes, the greatness of God is His ability to be great even in the face of our worst circumstances!

Twelve

GREAT LOVE

I was in Dallas, Texas at Soul's Harbor with Brother W.V. Grant, Sr. A great crusade was taking place. This particular night, a series of storms hit the area. Outside, golf ball size hail rained from the sky. Inside, I was just about to give an altar call. I noticed a young woman come in and sit in the back of the church. She was soaking wet. As the invitation was given, she made her way to the altar. The story of her life was about to change.

This woman was a prostitute, working the street in front of the church. She had been waiting for her pimp to pick her up when the storm hit. She thought she would seek refuge from the weather in the church. Instead, she found Refuge as she knelt in surrender to Jesus Christ. God, in His greatness, knew the precise time she would be standing outside the church and when I would be giving the invitation to come to the Lord. He chose this divine moment in time to save a prostitute.

God knows where you are at all times and He knows what you need. He knows the trials you are facing and the worries you struggle with each day. He's just waiting to be invited to help you in life's journey.

Ask and it will be given to you; seek and you will find; knock and the door will be opened to you.
MATTHEW 7:7

God's greatness provides for an answer to life. Without that assurance, I would never have been able to reach out and touch the hurting hearts of my generation. I know when I call upon God's name, He is going to answer and meet the need. He's our heavenly Father and demonstrates His great love to all His children.

Thirteen

HATTIE WILLS

The spring of the year around Kingsport, Tennessee is beautiful. The eastern Tennessee, southern Virginia region blooms in brilliant color amid the rolling mountains of Appalachian green. It was an inspirational backdrop to the revival meeting we were conducting. But thirty-five miles away in Greeneville, things were not so uplifting.

The Wills' family were long-time ministry supporters and friends. They were some of the first to help my wife and I when we began evangelizing. They had fed us, put us up in their home, and exhibited exceptional kindness and hospitality to us. Now we received the news from a friend that Miss Hattie Wills was dying.

It was three days before the Lord led me to go to pray for her. I took three other elders with me. The Wills' sisters were in the garden gathering fresh vegetables for dinner as we arrived. They excitedly invited us to share a meal, but I informed them I would not be eating. The other elders accepted their invitation and preparation for the meal was underway.

Inside, Miss Hattie was lying on the sofa. Tuberculosis had ravaged her already frail body. She was spitting up blood. I excused myself to the backyard and began praying. I waited for the Spirit to anoint me to minister healing to this faithful Sister. From inside the house, I heard them calling for everyone to come wash up for dinner. Just then, the Lord impressed me to anoint the dying woman and pray the prayer of faith before anyone ate. *"I'm going to raise her up and make her whole,"* the Spirit assured me.

The only problem was I had left my anointing oil back at the motel in Kingsport. So, we used cooking oil to fulfill the scripture in JAMES 5:14. I cursed the tuberculosis to come out of the infected lungs of the diminutive Miss Hattie. The power of God came upon her and she let out a scream. She jumped up from the sofa and was instantly and miraculously made whole! More than twenty years have passed since that memorable day. At this writing, Hattie is still alive and doing well. I believe in God's amazing healing power!

Fourteen

LONG DISTANCE?

I can't even remember the name of the little town in South Georgia. What I do remember is the little Baptist woman who came to the revival for healing in her body. The Lord met her at her point of need and she was healed. That part of this story is not unusual. Over the course of more than forty years of ministry, I believe I've seen just about every kind of sickness and disease healed. But this...

Years had gone by. This woman was suddenly afflicted with an incurable disease. Her family brought her to the hospital in Atlanta. She requested they try to find me to come and pray for her. They attempted to honor her request but couldn't reach me. I was in Canada at the time.

The day came when the doctor called the family together and informed them she only had a few hours left to live. She was already unconscious with merely a faint flicker of hope remaining. Grief-stricken, the family left the room to await the inevitable. The moments dragged on. Someone decided to open the door and check on their loved one. Unbelievably, she was now conscious and lucid! She lay there praising God for her miracle. But how could this be?

This woman began to relate to her family how Brother Walden had just come into the room to pray for her. The family exchanged puzzled looks. They had been standing just outside her hospital room in the hallway. No one had come in or left. The doctor was summoned to examine the patient. He couldn't find anything wrong with her. All her vital signs were normal. More tests were ordered. There was no sign of any debilitating disease. With a clean bill of health, she was sent home!

God is not limited to just one way of doing things. Apparently, God gave this woman a vision in which I came into the room and prayed for her. She believed if I prayed, she would receive a miracle. God somehow honored her faith, even though I was unavailable in Canada. But God is always available!

God is our refuge and strength, an ever-present help in trouble.

PSALM 46:1

Fifteen

THE GOD OF KNEE CAPS
AND PUPPY DOGS

We were conducting a crusade in Thomasville, Georgia. The power of God was present each night. God would anoint me to preach His Word and then He would confirm His Word by saving souls and setting the captive free.

One night a young woman came through the prayer line. She had a stiff leg. I customarily ask people what's wrong with them unless the Lord reveals it to me by His Spirit. She related the following story to the congregation.

A man had attacked and tried to kill her. While she was fighting for her life, his shotgun went off, exploding her kneecap. I asked to see her knee. There was no joint. Some people in the audience were dubious as I asked if they could believe with me for God to create a new kneecap in this woman's leg. I asked those who believed to raise their hands and stretch them toward us. We prayed together in faith. As we touched the heart of God in prayer, the Creator of all things touched this woman. Right before our eyes, we watched as a brand new kneecap formed!

She ran! She jumped! She couldn't contain her praise for the miraculous thing God had done!

Bolstered by the outstanding miracles that were taking place, the crowds began growing. Night after night, the altars swelled with people seeking God for salvation, healing, and deliverance. One evening, I looked into the audience and recognized a family. We had been friends for many years. I had baptized most of the family and they always attended our crusades when we were anywhere within driving distance. The grandmother approached me just before the service began. Her little grandson was by her side, sobbing uncontrollably.

Obviously upset, the grandmother told me what the problem was. As they were leaving the house to come to the crusade, a huge dog wandered into their yard and killed the boy's puppy. The puppy had been the center of this youngster's world. They were inseparable. He carried the puppy with him everywhere. As he napped, the puppy would lay at the foot of the bed and nap along with him.

The stray dog had attacked, viciously ripping the hide and crushing the fragile bones of this little puppy between its massive jaws. Blood was seeping out of the puppy's mouth and nose. All the horrified parents could do was place the carcass under the front porch and leave it for dead.

Through tearful sobs, this boy begged, "Bubba Walden, please pray for my puppy!" Trying to console the child, I told him I would pray for God to give him another puppy. The boy didn't want to hear this. Fresh tears streamed from his swollen eyes. He didn't want another puppy. He wanted his puppy.

I didn't know what to do so I gave in to his impossible request. "Okay son," I said, "Stop crying. I'll ask the Lord to heal your puppy." Before I finished praying, the boy's tears had subsided. But all during the service I kept thinking, "What is that child going to think if God doesn't heal his pet?" The Holy Spirit prompted me, *"Did you ask God to heal the puppy?"* I knew right then God would not let that little boy down.

The next night, here he came marching up to me with his grandmother in tow. He was grinning from ear to ear. He was so excited he could hardly talk. "Bubba Walden," he exclaimed, "When we got home last night, my puppy ran out from under the porch. He was yapping and jumping and wagging his tail!"

At this point the grandmother broke into the conversation. "As we pulled into the yard and saw the puppy, our grandson cried out 'Jesus did it, grandma! Jesus healed him!'" Remarkably, there wasn't any sign of the attack; not a trace of blood or even a scar on the puppy's body! I was reminded how Jesus taught His followers,

> *Unless you change and become like little children, you will never enter the kingdom of heaven.*
> MATTHEW 18:3B

Once again, He proved He is the God who moves whenever and wherever faith is found, whether in the heart of a child or someone a hundred years old.

Approximately twenty-two years passed since this happened and one day I ran into the boy's mother. She told me, "You know, my son still talks about the Lord raising his puppy from the dead!"

It's a miracle that boy, now an adult, will never forget. God loves all His creation. He made this world for all His creatures to live in and enjoy life. We serve an awesome God!

Sixteen

NEED A LITTLE "GET UP AND GO?"

The greatness of God often manifests itself in the strangest of ways and places. Each time, I am amazed at how the Lord accomplishes great things in these unusual situations.

I had been in Dallas, Texas in a crusade. One evening I felt compelled to take a walk after praying most of the afternoon. I dressed for church and, not knowing for sure where God wanted me to go, I just started walking. I strolled up the street. Nothing out of the ordinary happened. So I walked down another street. Everything there looked normal. But I still felt an urgency to keep walking. I headed back to my apartment waiting for something astounding to take place but everything appeared the same as when I had passed by before except for the presence of an elderly gentleman holding on to a street post. The Spirit of God quickened me. *"Stop and talk to him."*

I approached him. "Sir," I inquired, "How are you doing today?" As he turned to look at me, I could sense he was the reason I had been wearing out shoe leather.

"I used to be an air traffic controller," the gentleman began. "Then I got sick and was forced to retire. My wife passed away. My children grew up and moved out of town. They never come to see me anymore. I'm so lonely and I have no one to help me. My doctor says I'm not getting any better from this lung disease." He paused to catch his breath.

"This is the first time I've been out of the house in weeks because of my condition. Funny though, a little while ago I thought I heard a voice say 'Get up and go down to the street corner.' So I did. That's why I'm here and why I can hardly breathe. By the way, what business are you in?"

I responded by telling him I was a minister and that I must have heard the same voice he did. We began talking about Jesus and I had the privilege of leading him to salvation. I prayed and asked God to heal him, too. Still holding on to the street post, he stopped wheezing and began breathing normally! He thanked me and I watched as he made his way up the street. He was still praising God! And I am still amazed.

Seventeen

EVERY TRIBE, EVERY NATION

The revival at the Walpole Island Indian Reservation had lasted well into the night. It was now after eleven o'clock and our evangelistic team and I had not eaten. Every restaurant was closed but we kept driving, hoping to find something open.

Ahead, we spotted the faint glimmer of light coming from inside a Chinese restaurant. But as we stopped, the owner met us at the front door and explained they were closed for the night. I told him we were ministers and that we were very hungry. "There is a bar in the back," he offered. "It's open. There's a band and dancing going on. But if you don't mind eating there, I'll serve you."

I hesitated. The Holy Spirit said, *"Go!"*

I thanked the owner for his generosity and we proceeded back to the bar area. On the way, I casually mentioned how our evangelistic team had musicians and singers. We asked if, during the band's break, we could play and sing for the patrons and he indicated it was okay. Brother Jim sat down at the piano. He began playing and singing "Amazing Grace." A couple got up and started to dance until they realized it was a gospel song. They eased back into their seats. Meanwhile, I was busy witnessing to the bandleader. I found out the man was a backslidden Christian from Kentucky who had once been called to preach. His grandfather was a holiness minister. He cried as I prayed with him. We finished our meal and started to leave, but the owner wouldn't let us pay our bill. "You come back tomorrow," he insisted. "You can sing and talk."

The next night we sang and talked about Jesus there in the bar. The owner was excited. "Will you tell me more about Jesus? While you were speaking, I thought back to the time when I was a young boy in China. A missionary from the States took me to church and Sunday School."

The bar became a holy meeting place for that restaurant owner. I reintroduced him to the Lord Jesus and prayed with him to accept salvation. And another life was transformed by the greatness of God.

This reminds me of the time we were having revival in the ballroom of the Balmoral Hotel in Winnipeg, Manitoba. The hotel's owner was Jewish. We had been there three days when he sent word he wanted to talk to me. I went up to his room. The man was eighty years old.

"I want to ask you a question," he began.

"Okay," I countered.

"I've been hiding in the kitchen at night listening to you speak. What makes you so different from the other preachers who rent the ballroom from us?"

I began to share the simple story of the great love of God; how God loved the world so much that He gave His only begotten Son to die on Calvary for him. I led him to heartfelt salvation. He encountered the God of Abraham, Isaac, and Jacob and the Lord of every tribe and nation. His greatness extends to everyone regardless of ethnic background, social status, or the size of their bank account.

The LORD does not look at the things man looks at. Man looks at the outward appearance, but the LORD looks at the heart.

I SAMUEL 16:7B

Eighteen

WHEN DEATH MEETS LIFE

What do you do when someone drops dead right in the middle of your preaching? I don't mean "almost" dead. This individual dropped "graveyard" dead; the kind of dead you ship to the funeral home and bury. In the confusion, someone managed to call an ambulance. The man had been dead about twenty minutes when someone suggested I go pray for him.

Brother Curtis Allbritten and myself knelt over his lifeless body. We didn't know what to say, so we kept repeating, "O God, heal him and raise him up." I'm not sure how long this went on but suddenly the Spirit of the Lord spoke to me. *"You don't raise the dead like you pray for the sick. Command the spirit of life to return back into his body."*

By this time, the ambulance siren cascaded through the door of the church. A nurse checked for his pulse. Nothing. There were no signs of life. His eyes were rolled back into his head. I felt the sticky sweat associated with death on his exposed skin. But it didn't matter because I had just heard directly from God.

I commanded his spirit to come back into his body and the man rose to his feet as the paramedics were bringing the gurney through the front doors! Hallelujah, the Lord's greatness is bigger than death! Raising the dead is outstanding enough but there is, (as a famous radio commentator would say), more to this story...

Several years before, I had left Atlanta, Georgia with $15.00 in my pocket. I guess that would have been fine if I was on my way to Tennessee. But I was driving to my first revival in Canada. Cold weather had crept into the South this month of January and the roads were solid ice from Chattanooga to Toronto. Interstate 75 hadn't been constructed yet and the driving was treacherous as we traversed over the frozen Appalachian mountain range. I imagine it would be next to impossible to head out with just $15.00 today, even with good roads and ideal conditions, but by faith and the grace of God, we did it then.

Upon arriving, my clothes needed attention so I decided to take them to the dry cleaners. After placing all my clothes with the cleaners, it dawned on me I didn't have any money to get them back out. I was forced to wear the same suit from Sunday to the following Friday. And by the time Friday rolled around, the congregation didn't have to wonder where I was...they could smell me coming!

I hadn't received any offerings and I didn't know what I was going to do. We were staying with the pastor in his home and they were feeding us all we wanted to eat but that didn't get my clothes out of the cleaners. But that Friday night, a little girl walked up to me and put $20.00 in my hand and whispered, "God told me to give this to you."

The next day, my first order of business was to go to the cleaners. You know, often it doesn't take everybody to meet somebody's need. It just takes someone who is faithful and wants to be blessed by obeying God. Later I discovered this little girl was the daughter of the man who had been raised from the dead during the Indian reservation revival! I could end the story here but there's still more...

Years went by and I hadn't heard anything from this "miracle family." While back in Canada for a camp meeting, someone mentioned the little girl had grown up and studied nursing. She then married and was serving as a missionary in Iceland. I rejoiced because she had chosen to use her skills to help people and share the gospel with them! But another chapter in God's greatness was still waiting to unfold...

We conducted a "School of Champions" training center in Georgia. One of our former graduates told me about a friend of hers, a Sister Crosby, who was in the hospital in London, Ontario. This woman had called and requested I get in touch with her to pray for her healing. I waited two days before calling. I sought the Lord in prayer. The third day, I felt an urgency to call her number at the hospital. I called directly to her room and asked to speak to Mrs. Crosby. There was no one there by that name.

"There has to be," I stated. "She left this number for me to call and pray for her because she is sick." The supervising nurse came on the line and informed me that the woman I was attempting to reach had checked out the day before.

Now, if you don't know you are in the will of God, your first thought would probably be 'I blew it. I must have missed God.' But I knew I had heard from the Lord so I asked the nurse if I could talk to the patient who was in the room.

In a moment a voice responded, "Hello?"

I began by relating I was a minister and was supposed to call this number to pray for a woman.

"I'm not sure if the names have been mixed up or the rooms switched but the message said it was an emergency. Are you sure you're not Mrs. Crosby?"

The voice on the other end began sobbing. "No, I'm not her. I'm a missionary. I've had to come home from the mission field because of an illness."

I made the comment I was from Georgia and she started crying harder.

"I was praying just a few minutes before this phone rang. I asked God if He had to have someone from Georgia call, please just have them ring this number and pray the prayer of faith for me!"

So I prayed the prayer of faith. And God restored this lady's health so she could return to her mission work...in Iceland! Amazingly, **IT WAS THE SAME GIRL WHOSE FATHER WAS RAISED FROM THE DEAD AND WHO HAD BLESSED ME WITH $20.00 SO I COULD GET MY SUITS OUT OF THE CLEANERS!**

That's the end of this great story but not the greatness of God. Reflecting back over these events, it proves God is faithful to keep his promises.

And if anyone gives even a cup of cold water to one of these little ones because he is my disciple, I tell you the truth, he will certainly not lose his reward.
MATTHEW 10:42

What more can you possibly say about God other than, HE IS GREAT!

Nineteen

IN THE PRESENCE OF GREATNESS

Were my eyes playing tricks on me? I looked again and there it was; a glow of light shining over this man. Out of three thousand people under the gospel tent, the Lord had singled out this one person to me.

I was in Clearwater, Florida with LeRoy Jenkins in a tent meeting. Standing at one end of the tent, I observed the man with the halo in this vast audience of people. *"Go fasten yourself to this man,"* the Spirit instructed. I didn't understand what the Lord was speaking to me but, in obedience, I walked up to him and introduced myself.

Brother Dennis Holt was in the used car business. The night I met him, God spoke and told him to make sure I had a car to drive as long as I preached the Word. What he didn't know was my wife and I had just entered into full-time ministry with no more than $200.00 to our name. God blessed him for his commitment and God blessed me through his faithfulness. Now, thirty-eight years later, he still makes sure I don't have to walk wherever I go to spread the gospel.

A number of years after we first met, I decided to set up the tent in Brother Holt's hometown of Greeneville, Tennessee. He asked if I could go by and visit with an old friend of his who ran a service station. It so happened the tent was located just up the road from the station and so I promised to check on his acquaintance.

I walked into the station and was greeted by a group of men sitting around an old pot-bellied heater. They were chewing tobacco and playing checkers. I asked to meet Ross Luttrell. Ross got up and shook my hand as I told him of our mutual friend and why I was in Greeneville.

Ross mentioned he had seen our advertising in the newspaper and was intrigued by the claim 'the blind see, the deaf hear, and the lame walk.' You see, Ross had arthritis. Hard, gristle knots the size of golf balls protruded from his joints.

"What can you do for this?" he asked skeptically as he showed me his crippling condition.

"Well, I can pray and believe the Lord will heal you," I announced in faith. I dropped to my knees, closed my eyes, and began to pray. I'm not sure what the rest of those men thought, but shortly I heard Ross begin to cry. When I opened my eyes, God had healed him completely!

I didn't need any more advertising. Ross Luttrell took care of that for me. As people stopped for gas or repairs at his service station, he would 'show and tell' everyone what had happened. The tent filled.

One evening, just before going to the platform to minister, I stood outside the tent looking up at the stars. The night air was hot and still, not a cloud in the sky, and the heavens radiated with twinkling lights. "What a beautiful night!" I thought to myself. I heard the congregation singing "Only Believe" and so I left my reveling in God's greatness and made my way to the platform. In the crowd, thirty people in stretchers and wheelchairs were anticipating their miracle that night. I hadn't even begun preaching when I noticed the tent foreman scurrying to let down the side curtains. "What is he up to?" I wondered.

Suddenly, the tent began flapping. People jumped to their feet, shouting and praising God. Those standing on the outside perimeter of the canvas cathedral crawled to the altar in repentance. For the next half hour, the ensuing commotion filled the tent with dry, Tennessee dust. And when it was all over, everyone was healed including all thirty who were infirm and crippled. They left their stretchers and wheelchairs behind!

People who lived nearby where the tent was located told me later what had happened. They had watched as a bright cloud appeared from out of the west and settled directly over the tent! It hovered over our gathering for approximately thirty minutes and then lifted and disappeared in the east!

A young Sister approached me after one of the morning services. She had received the infilling of the Holy Spirit and her zeal was evident. "The Lord has spoken to me for you and some of the Brothers to go and pray for a man I know who is in a wheelchair. He lives about fifteen miles out in the country. Will you come?" she asked excitedly.

I prayed about it and waited a few days. Then we all got together and headed out to the man's house. There was no one home when we arrived so we waited. And waited. Three hours passed. Finally, the Sister said, "The Lord just reminded me of a girl in her twenties who has rheumatoid arthritis. She can't even get out of bed by herself. She lives just up the road from here." We were tired of sitting and waiting so we decided to go pray for her.

The girl was a pitiful sight. Her body lay rigid on the bed. She was unable to sit up in a regular chair so her family had designed a reclining seat for her. They moved her into it from the bed. But her stiffened and deformed condition hadn't dampened her spirit. "I love God with all my heart," she said. And for the next thirty minutes I listened intently to every word she spoke.

"I would be so grateful to God if He would just heal me so I could sit in the grass, smell the flowers, and feel a cool breeze blowing through my hair," she sighed dreamily. And as God is my witness, the Holy Spirit filled the room as she uttered those words. *"Now is the time to pray,"* the Spirit commanded.

I prayed and her bones began to pop and crack. Then she stood to her feet! When this young girl realized what had happened, she walked over to the front door. It was a beautiful spring day. Outside the grass was a lush, olive green. The flowers were bursting with color. You could smell the fresh scent of new life in the mountain air. She stood for a moment gazing at a world she hadn't been able to enjoy for such a long time. Then, without a word, she walked into the yard and sat down in the grass. The breeze gently sifted her hair. She sat praising God with her hands raised toward heaven, a widening smile on her face, and tears of joy trickling from her eyes. Not wanting to disturb such a divinely powerful moment, we slipped away. I watched her until we drove out of sight.

My heart was overflowing with joy. I caught a fleeting sense of what the psalmist David must have felt when he penned, "My cup overflows (PSALM 23:5)."

We stopped back by the house where we had been waiting for over three hours for the man we had originally come to pray for. He was still not home. The scripture came to mind,

Can you fathom the mysteries of God? Can you probe the limits of the Almighty? They are higher than the heavens - what can you do? They are deeper than the depths of the grave - what can you know?
JOB 11:7-8

Had this man been at home, we might not have seen God work a miracle for the young lady. However, God made the arrangements and in His impeccable timing we discovered how perfect His greatness is!

Twenty

GOD'S GAZE
OF GRACE

The eyes of the Lord are always upon us. No matter
where we go or what we are doing, the eyes of our heavenly
Father are watching.

> *From heaven the LORD looks down and sees all*
> *mankind; from his dwelling place he watches all who*
> *live on earth - he who forms the hearts of all, who*
> *considers everything they do. But the eyes of the LORD*
> *are on those who fear him, on those whose hope is in his*
> *unfailing love.*
>
> PSALM 33:13-15,18

To a child of God, this realization brings peace in
every storm of life. It's also important to me as a minister
because I have found, you don't have to invite trouble.
Trouble seems to show up when you least expect it.

I had just finished ministering one night when the
Holy Spirit impressed me, *"There is someone here who is*
planning to take their life." I conveyed to the congregation
what the Spirit had spoken to me. A young woman stood

up and came to the front. As we began to pray for her, she began to thrash about violently. It took several strong men to subdue this seemingly harmless woman.

After we cast out the demon spirit that controlled this woman, she made a startling confession. A voice had spoken to her to come to the meeting with a knife, to kill me as I left the tent, and then take her own life. But God's watchful eye knew the enemy's evil intentions. God's greatness provided protection for me and brought deliverance for this young woman. She left the meeting free of her sins and delivered from the demonic influence over her mind!

In this same meeting, we also heard an amazing testimony from a truck driver.

"When I left home for a trip to Louisiana to pick up my cargo, everything seemed to be wonderful. I had hugged and kissed my wife and children goodbye and as far as I knew, there were no problems. I hated to leave my family, but driving a truck was all I had ever done. In fact, I was driving trucks when my wife and I got married.

While in Louisiana, my wife called me and said she didn't love me anymore. It broke my heart. I had never had anything hurt me so bad. I thought I would lose my mind because I love my family. Sitting behind the wheel of my rig, I began praying and headed home. I didn't know what else to do.

About 3:30 AM, something impressed me to turn on the radio. A familiar voice filled the cab of my eighteen-wheeler. Brother Walden preached a message that was just what I needed to hear at this low point in my life. At the end of the broadcast, Brother Walden invited listeners to attend this campmeeting. The Lord told me to come here and have Brother Walden pray for me. I've driven 500 miles just to be here."

After hearing his testimony, I knew everything would work out between he and his wife. How could I be so positive? I knew he had definitely heard from God. You see, I've never been on the radio in that part of the country or anywhere else at that time in the morning. How or why I was preaching on the radio at that specific time is still a mystery but the eyes of the Lord were on that man. When most people were sleeping, a watchful and vigilant God was concerned about the broken heart of a truck driver. We prayed together and he left with faith that the Lord was going to put his life back together.

From time to time, we all suffer pain. Sometimes pain affects us physically. But there is a pain that comes from unkind words. It's a pain that doesn't bleed or leave outward scars. All the medication in the world cannot alleviate this kind of pain. Only the greatness of God can bring healing and mend the pieces of a torn life. His eyes see you at the point of your need and He is big enough for,

The eyes of the LORD are on the righteous and his ears are attentive to their cry. The righteous cry out, and the LORD hears them; he delivers them from all their troubles. The LORD is close to the brokenhearted and saves those who are crushed in spirit. A righteous man may have many troubles, but the LORD delivers him from them all.

PSALM 34:15,17-19

Twenty-One

THE CITY OF BROTHERLY LOVE

A good friend of mine called and asked me to stop by the church he was pastoring and preach for him before I continued on into Canada. Brother Nathan Bennett had helped me when I first began in the ministry, so I made the commitment to come to Philadelphia. The church was downtown on Broad Street next to the hotel where I was to stay.

One evening, about an hour before service time, the Holy Spirit interrupted my praying. Now, I always try to be sensitive to what the Spirit of God says to me. Many times it is very specific and He reveals detail by detail what He wants me to do. Other times, it is more like a directive. This was one of those times. *"Go, stand on the sidewalk and wait,"* the Spirit impressed me. *"I will send him to you and you will show My love to him."*

I glanced out the window. Silver-dollar size snowflakes hung suspended in the frigid February air. But obediently, I bundled myself up in my warmest coat and headed downstairs. I'll be the first to admit...when you're cold and wet and waiting for whatever, time seems to stop. I waited. Five minutes passed ever so slowly, then ten, fifteen, and thirty. I tried to stay warm. Forty-five endless minutes of standing on the deserted sidewalk and not a soul came up to me. What was I going to do? The church service had already begun and I knew any minute I would have to abandon my post. Then I heard the Holy Spirit speak again. *"There's the man you've been waiting on."*

I peered through the darkness and the falling snow across Broad Street and saw him. My anticipation warmed as the man started across the street. As he got about halfway across the road, he stopped, turned, and headed back in the opposite direction! I got cold again. I didn't know what to do so I just stood there watching him disappear into the night. "What's that, Lord? I thought You said he was the one."

Suddenly, he turned again and headed back in my direction. This time he crossed over Broad Street, came over to where I was standing, and asked if I could spare some change for a cup of coffee. It didn't take any discernment to see he was as cold as I was. My eyes fell to the pair of worn-out shoes that were failing miserably at keeping his feet from the elements. I expected a hard-luck story but I really wasn't prepared for what I was about to hear.

"I've just been released from jail," he explained. "I thought I'd go home to my wife and kids but she turned me away. She wouldn't let me come inside to see the children. So I figured I could stay at my mother's house but when I got there, she acted as though I wasn't her son. My own momma wouldn't even have anything to do with me! I don't want to live like this," he continued, "But I don't know what to do."

By this time you could hear the sounds of "Only Believe" coming from inside the church. It's been my theme song for over forty years now and it signals me to the platform to minister. So I motioned him toward the church entrance. "I'm a preacher," I told him, "And I'm speaking in there tonight. If you will go with me, when the service is over, I'll buy you a hot meal." He nodded. Or maybe he was shivering. But he followed me inside.

I finished preaching that night and gave an altar call. He was the first one to the front. The Lord gloriously saved his soul and filled him with the Holy Spirit. Now that his inner man was right, it was time for the outer man to get a much-needed makeover. The deacons of that church got together and put the man in a nice hotel room, fed him, and had him fitted for a new suit of clothes with a new pair of shoes. He came back the next night looking like a Philadelphia lawyer. That man not only became a faithful church member, he was restored to his family, and later served as a deacon in that assembly.

All because a great God chose a chilly night in February to demonstrate His greatness at the lowest point in a forsaken man's life!

Twenty-Two

THE LONG ARM OF GOD'S MERCY

God often does great things after dark. Now I didn't say He operates in darkness because God is light and in Him there is no darkness at all (1 JOHN 1:5). No, while the rest of His creation is sleeping, God is still "on call" and showing off His untiring greatness.

Nothing much was stirring early that morning. We were on the final leg of our journey back to Georgia from a revival in New Brunswick, Canada. Myself and another Brother had alternated driving the 1,100 miles. Stopping only to eat and refuel our van, we were tired and anticipating getting home to our families. I was lying down in the back to get some rest. I awoke when I felt our vehicle slow to a stop. Thinking we had finally arrived, I sat up and looked out the window. We were not home. I blinked a few times and glanced at the time on my watch. 3:27 AM. It took just a few more moments and the flashing blue lights for me to figure out why we had stopped. The cool, night air poured through the driver's side window as the Brother with me waited to present his license to the uniformed officer.

"Were you speeding?" I questioned him.

"No," he replied. "I'm not sure why we've been pulled over."

So we both sat there quietly waiting for an explanation from the policeman.

"You gentlemen are out mighty late, aren't you?"

Whether it was a question or a definitive statement I don't know. But I thought, how many times have you ever been pulled over for being out late at night? The only thing my tired brain could rationalize was that this policeman was just overly suspicious of any activity in his sleepy little community. I looked around. Everything was dark and quiet. The officer was inspecting the license and vehicle registration.

"So where are you'all heading so late at night?"

Brother Erich explained we were on our way home to Conyers and then proceeded to tell him we had driven for two days from a revival meeting in Canada.

"You're from Conyers? I've been meaning to look up a preacher in Conyers," he commented. "You wouldn't happen to know a Rev. Franklin Walden, would you?"

A look of surprise came over Brother Erich. He pointed over at me. "That's him right there!"

It was the officer's turn to look surprised. He appeared stunned at this sudden turn of events. In the middle of the night on a lonely stretch of Georgia country road, God's greatness was at work.

The man began telling me a tragic and heart-wrenching story. He had been a lay pastor in a nearby church while continuing his job as a police officer. One day he had come home and inadvertently left his service revolver lying on the bed. His four year-old child came into the room and began playing with the still-loaded weapon. The boy pulled the trigger, instantly killing himself. The father was grief-stricken and overwhelmed with guilt. He resigned the pastorate. His job became a struggle. His marriage deteriorated. Thoughts of suicide constantly plagued his mind. He hadn't been able to reconcile his son's death or bring himself to seek counseling and help. But God had heard the cry of his heart and made arrangements for this "chance" meeting.

All the tiredness left my body. My heart went out to this despondent man and the burden he had been carrying. I felt the powerful compassion of the Holy Spirit as I shared with him the love of God. The tears streaming down his face gave evidence that God's mercy was purging the dark shadows of his life and lifting the heavy shroud of guilt to allow healing to come to his soul and mind. We joined hands in prayer on the side of the road. The air was electric with the magnitude of what God was accomplishing in this divine moment in time.

The policeman's facial expression showed the relief from the strain and pressure of the months following his tragedy. He thanked me and we thanked God together for His mighty, delivering power. Then he wished us well on our remaining miles home.

"And, by the way, there's no ticket."

We drove the rest of the way home in awe, marveling at the greatness of a God who can turn midnight to day.

For God, who said, 'Let light shine out of darkness,' made his light shine in our hearts to give us the light of the knowledge of the glory of God in the face of Christ. But we have this treasure in jars of clay to show that this all-surpassing power is from God and not from us. We are hard pressed on every side, but not crushed; perplexed, but not in despair; persecuted, but not abandoned; struck down, but not destroyed.
2 CORINTHIANS 4:6-9

Twenty-Three

DOGGONE-IT

I really enjoy walking to King's Grocery store and down by the river. For me, it's good exercise and you never know what great things you might encounter as you get outdoors into God's creation. Take this morning, for example. I had walked about a mile when I saw a happy sight. A mother dog and her puppies were playing along a side street. They were having a great time together. "Now that's how a family should be," I thought. If families could enjoy each other and be happy together, there wouldn't be any family problems that they couldn't work out among themselves.

For about a week I would look for this four-legged family every time my walks took me into town. Sometimes the puppies would be nursing, snuggled close to their protective mother. Often they would be down by the railroad tracks playing and having a wonderful time. This particular day was absolutely perfect. The sun was shining; it wasn't too hot or too cold, just a beautiful day for a nice, leisurely walk. And there were the puppies with their mother, enjoying the day God had made just as I was.

An hour later, though, as I made my way back home I saw a terrible scene. There were no playful yelps, no teasing bites and rolling through the grass. The mother was lying at the edge of the road. Her paws were crossed. Her head was lying across her paws, her eyes sad and distant. I thought my heart would break. Evidently, an automobile had run over her puppies and they lay motionless in the street. The mother had been powerless to save them from this unexpected danger and now she lay grieving the loss of her family. I felt her pain and as I turned to leave, I said a prayer for the mother dog. My soul was filled with a sudden understanding. The Holy Spirit revealed to me that God made all living creatures to feel pain and loss down to the very core of their being. God created everything with emotion.

Another week passed and I decided to take a morning walk down to the river. A cool breeze was rustling the leaves, the birds were singing, and I was distinctly aware of God's presence. Quietly I began thanking the Lord for His many blessings. But I couldn't help thinking about the last time I had been walking. The image of the broken-hearted mother dog was still vivid in my mind, along with the realization of how quickly joy can turn into sadness. As I walked along, I knew I had not been as thankful to God as I should be for all He had done in my life.

Suddenly, my thoughts were jarred by something that had bumped against the back of my legs. Was it perhaps a pebble I had accidentally kicked up? I looked down but couldn't see anything unusual. I took a few more steps and it happened again. I whirled around and looked behind me. I still didn't see anything. Puzzled, I stared down at the ground and there, between my feet, was a puppy. It was so small. "How in the world did this puppy wind up way out here?" I mused. My house was the closest residence and it was a little more than a mile away. I couldn't just leave him there beside the road. I imagined him getting run over like...

So I reached down and petted the tiny bundle of fur. My mind drifted to the time we had given my five year-old son, Franklin Jr., a collie. The whole family loved the dog very much, but we were unable to keep her for long. My wife and I had decided we would never again be responsible for a dog. So what did I do? I let this handful of puppy follow me home!

I believe the Lord gave that little puppy to me. When I got home I justified my actions to my wife by telling her the dog was a "stranger" and I "took him in," hoping the scriptural intonation would soften her to the idea of a new pet. At times he does get in the way of things but the little mutt is the most intelligent creature I've ever seen. When I grab a walking stick for my daily jaunt, he'll pick up a stick and carry it between his teeth. He'll look up at me as if to say, "Hey, I can do that too." My wife was cleaning around the yard, picking up pine cones. He watched briefly, then began collecting pine cones and bringing them to her.

A minister friend of mine came to visit. He was recovering from a stroke and so he had his physical therapist along when he stopped by the house. The two of them were out walking so Brother Croft could exercise and regain control of his mobility. Amos tagged along behind them as they made their way along the fenced boundary of the yard. There was a small tree branch lying close to the fence directly in their path. That dog saw the obstruction and ran ahead to drag it away so Brother Croft wouldn't trip over it!

Now he's learned a new trick. We have a security light that comes on when the motion detector is activated. You know how it works; when something walks through that certain area, it triggers the light. Amos knows where that "zone" is. One night there was a noise outside the house. Amos alerted us by barking and then ran to where he could trigger the motion detector. Even the dog knew it was good to "put a little light on the subject!"

I believe we should love and enjoy everything God brings into our lives. And if we could just love one another as He has loved us, this world would be filled with joy unspeakable and glory. Isn't it wonderful to know God loves us even when we are unlovable and no one else seems to care? His love is greater than we can ever imagine!

Twenty-four

THE MINISTRY OF HEALING

People have asked me over the years, "How and when did you know you were chosen by God to pray for the sick?" I believe every born-again believer has the right to pray for the sick and see them healed. But I also believe there are some, like me, whom God anoints for special ministries into which He has called them. For example, my dad was one of the greatest men of faith I have ever known. As I was growing up, I saw many people healed by the power of God as dad would anoint them with oil and pray the prayer of faith.

We lived in the country and only went to town on Saturdays. It was one of those Saturdays when we met with the local bank president. He told dad he had been suffering with a persistent migraine for three days. The bank was bustling with the local towns' people. Dad just reached into his pocket and got out his small vial of anointing oil. "Mr. Sims," he said, "There's no need for you to have that headache any longer." He anointed Mr. Sims with the oil, prayed right there in the middle of all those people, and the banker was instantly healed!

We left the bank and were greeted by the Chief of Police on the street corner. "How are you today, Mr. Mitchell?" my father inquired.

"Sam," he replied, "I think I'm going to have to retire. My arthritis has gotten so bad, I can hardly walk."

"You don't have to retire. You're the best chief we've had," dad stated.

And out came the bottle of oil from his overalls. He anointed Chief Mitchell and the man was healed right then and there! He remained Chief of Police and lived well into his seventies.

My father was never considered a pastor, evangelist, or one of the five-fold ministry (EPHESIANS 4:11-12). He just loved the Lord and believed God answered his prayers!

I felt God wanted me to preach the gospel when I had my first vision at the age of twelve. But it wasn't until many years later that I knew God had called me into a healing ministry.

I was in Mills, Kentucky in a revival. I had made my way to a secluded place on the mountain and remained there the whole day, praying for the meeting that night. Leaning back against a large rock, I let my mind wander to those who were coming to be healed in the service. Suddenly, a cloud appeared through the trees. It covered the spot where I had come to seek the Lord. His voice spoke to my inner being. *"You will have a healing ministry from this day on."* As quickly as it had appeared, the cloud lifted and disappeared.

Words cannot express what I felt being in God's presence that way. I left that mountain retreat so full of joy! I had the abiding confidence I was going to see suffering people made whole.

That night, I prayed for a man who had only one lung. The other had been removed because of "black lung," a common occurrence among those who had worked many years in the coal mines. He had come for prayer because his only working lung was now diseased as well. I prayed the prayer of faith and believed God had healed him.

The following day we left and came home to Georgia. Three weeks later, I got a letter from this man. He had gone back to his doctor for a check-up. After the x-rays, the doctor had rushed back into the examining room. "You're not the same man I operated on five years ago. I know you say you are but you can't be!" he exclaimed. More x-rays were ordered. The results were the same as the first set. This man asked the doctor what the problem was. The surgeon had a startling revelation.

"The last time I examined you, you had one removed lung and a hole in your remaining lung. Today, these x-rays show two healthy lungs. Best of all, there is no sign of any "black lung!" He placed the x-rays up against the light. "I don't know what's happened to you, but you have two perfect lungs!"

God is not only the healer but He is the Creator of all things. He can work with what you have. But even if it is missing, He can create a new one! And it's just a prayer away!

Twenty-five

CONCLUSION

Can we fully understand the greatness of God? It's a question I still ask myself. We can obviously see, hear, smell, taste, and touch the power of His handiwork throughout creation. Our five senses bring us closer to the realization of a Supreme Being. But it is only through the work of Christ in our inner being, where our understanding begins to comprehend how great God really is!

When God's Spirit lives within us, we begin looking at what He has made through different eyes. We will even have a change of attitude and appreciate things we've never noticed before because the greatness of God appears in some of the most unusual settings. He reveals His greatness for one reason - to cause us to be in unique fellowship with God through His love for us. Consider the Biblical references to an individual who possibly had the most special and unique relationship with God ever recorded.

Enoch walked with God; then he was no more, because God took him away.
GENESIS 5:24

For before he was taken, he was commended as one who pleased God. And without faith it is impossible to please

God, because anyone who comes to him must believe that he exists and that he rewards those who earnestly seek him.

HEBREWS 11:5-6

God's greatness is revealed to our five senses where we can know He exists, but it is up to us to respond to His greatness in order for a bond of fellowship to be made.

Look at the life of the shepherd boy turned king. Throughout David's writings in the Psalms, we read his constant praises as he observed the created work of the Lord. And one of the greatest compliments a person can receive is that David was a man after God's own heart (ACTS 13:22). We can glean from this scripture that the thing that pleased God so much about David was his recognition of God's greatness and his desire to serve Him as a result.

God is a Spirit and His Spirit lives in every born-again child of God. The Bible tells us His Spirit will guide us in all spiritual truth so we can build a relationship with our heavenly Father. His Spirit opens up the mind of Christ to us so we can know the will of God for our lives. It allows us to grow in wisdom and understanding. It challenges us to set our goals higher than what we can achieve here on earth. Our representation of Christ is exemplified by reaching out to those with hurting hearts and showing them the love and greatness of God.

My joy comes from knowing the Father is pleased with me when I exercise my faith in Him. I have put my faith to work by ministering to others. The process of sharing with others releases the greatness of God. My daily desire is to tell someone about our caring, heavenly Father